GABRIEL YARED

DUETS FOR CELLO

T0085450

A CLOCHE-PIED 2
ANDANTE 3
BALADE SUR L'EAU 4
BARCAROLLE 6
BORDEAUX MENTHE 8
IMPROVISATION 10
ELÉGIE 13
LE BEAU RÔLE 14
LE HÉRISSON 16
PETITE MARCHE 17
PAS DE DEUX 18
PETITE ETUDE 20

PIZZICATI 22
PRÉLUDE 24
PROCESSION 26
PIÈCE LYRIQUE 28
QUESTIONS RÉPONSES 29
STACCATO LEGATO 30
TANGOCELLO 32
UN ADIEU 34
TARANTELLE 35
VALSE DE LORETTA 38

CD TRACK LISTING 40

Published by
Chester Music Limited
14-15 Berners Street, London W1T 3LJ, UK.

Exclusive Distributors:
Music Sales Limited
Distribution Centre, Newmarket Road, Bury St Edmunds, Suffolk IP33 3YB, UK.
Music Sales Pty Limited
20 Resolution Drive, Caringbah, NSW 2229, Australia.

Order No. CH78023
ISBN: 978-1-84938-923-5
This book © Copyright 2011 Chester Music Limited.

Composed by Gabriel Yared.
CDs recorded, mixed and mastered by Jonas Persson & David Menke.
Cellos: Sarah Jacob, Julie Sevilla, Martin Loveday & John Heley.
Edited by Ann Barkway & David Menke.
Music processed by Paul Ewers Music Design.

Printed in the EU.

www.musicsales.com

CHESTER MUSIC
PART OF THE MUSIC SALES GROUP
London/New York/Paris/Sydney/Copenhagen/Berlin/Madrid/Hong Kong/Tokyo

A Cloche-Pied

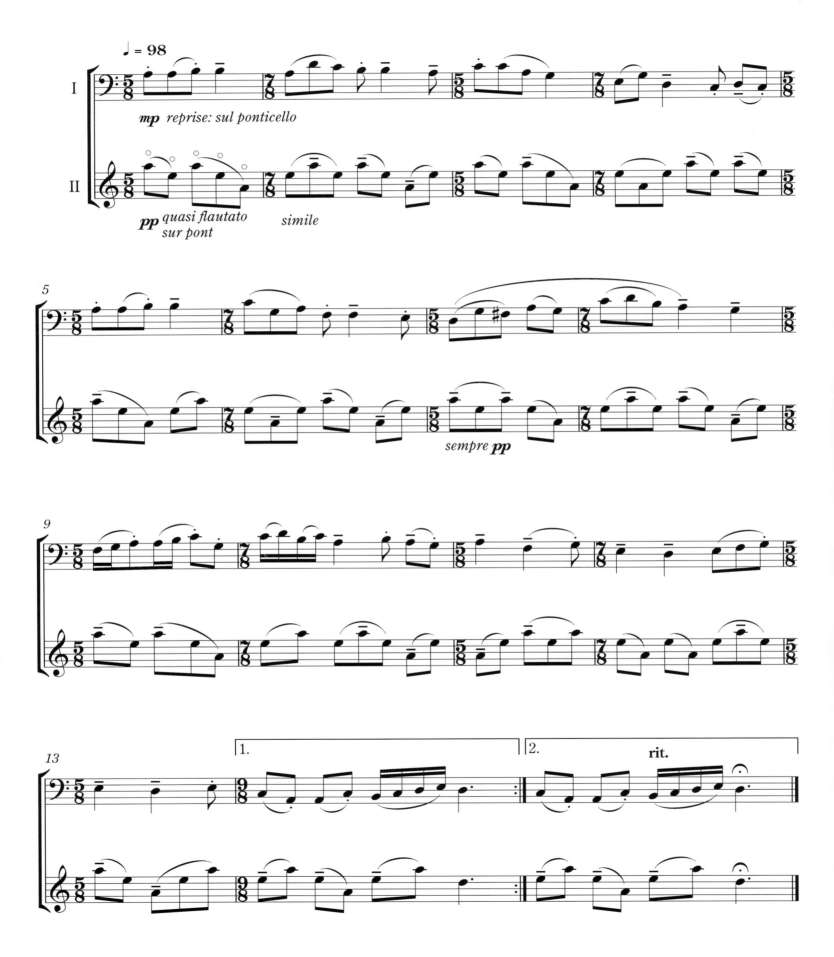

Andante

Balade sur l'Eau

D.C. al Fine
A tempo primo

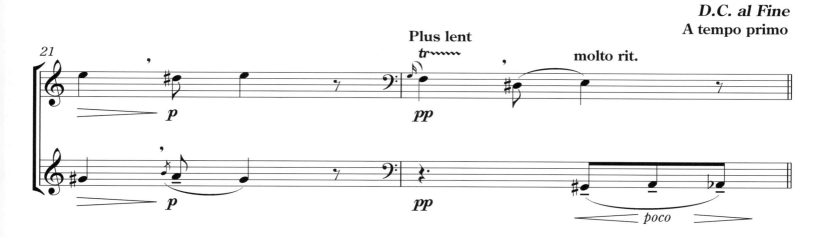

Barcarolle

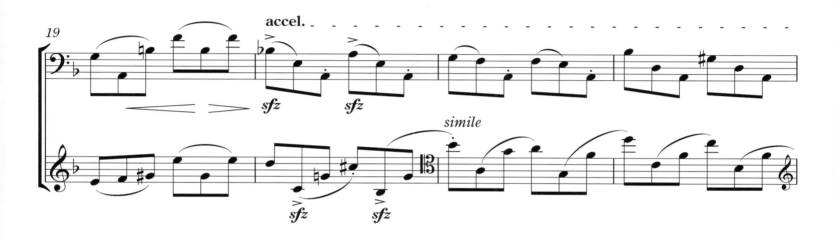

Bordeaux Menthe

Improvisation

Elégie

Le Beau Rôle

Andante e cantando (♩ = 54)

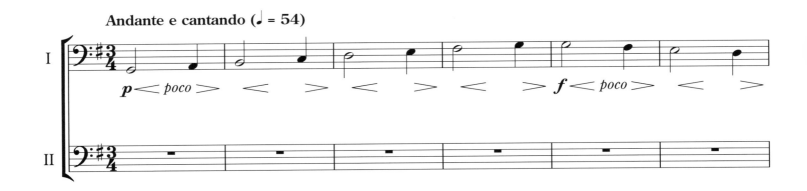

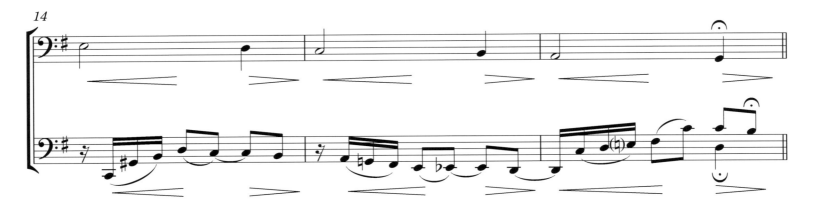

Le Hérisson

Petite Marche

Pas de Deux

Petite Etude

GABRIEL YARED

DUETS FOR CELLO

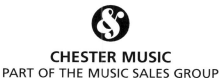

D.C. al Fine
A tempo primo

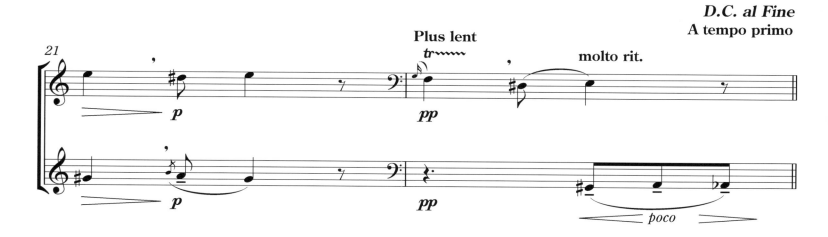

Barcarolle

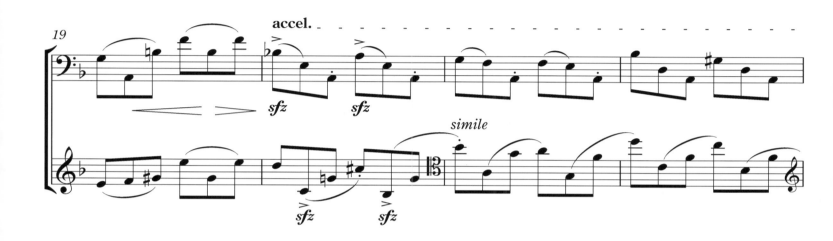

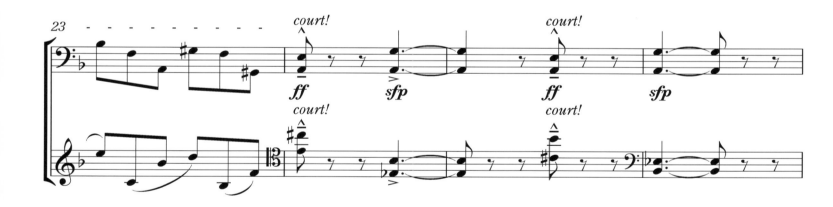

Bordeaux Menthe

9

Improvisation

Elégie

Le Beau Rôle

Le Hérisson

Petite Marche

Pas de Deux

Petite Etude

molto rall.

a tempo (ou un peu plus lent)

Pizzicati

Prélude

Procession

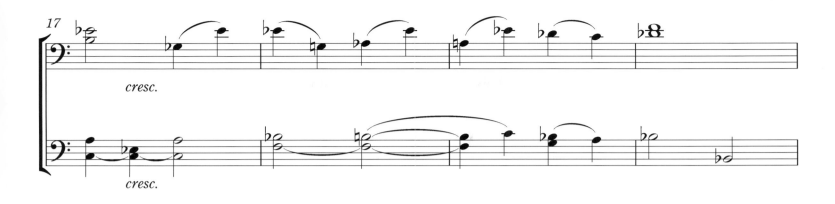

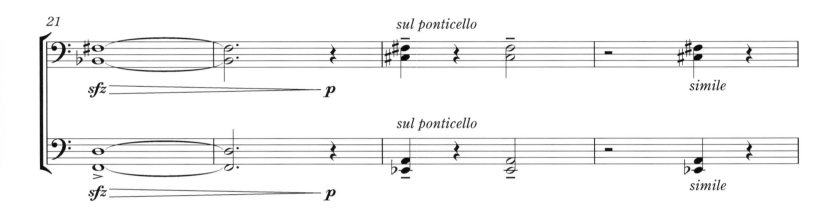

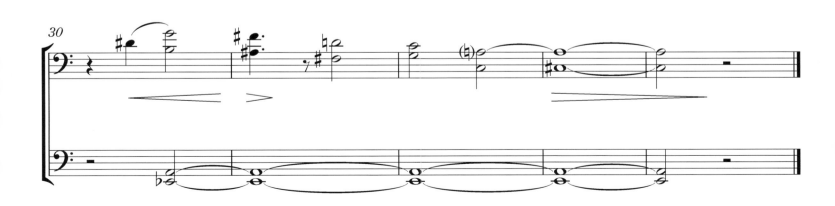

Pièce Lyrique

Questions Réponses

Staccato Legato

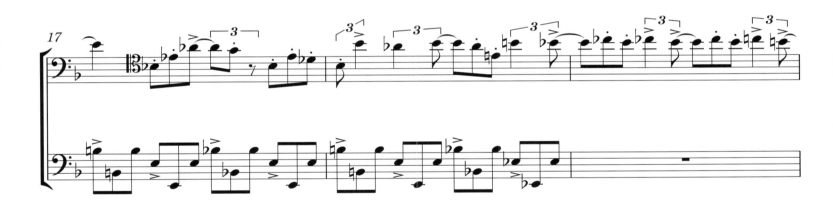

TangoCello

Un Adieu

Tarantelle

Slightly faster

Valse de Loretta

Pizzicati

Prélude

Procession

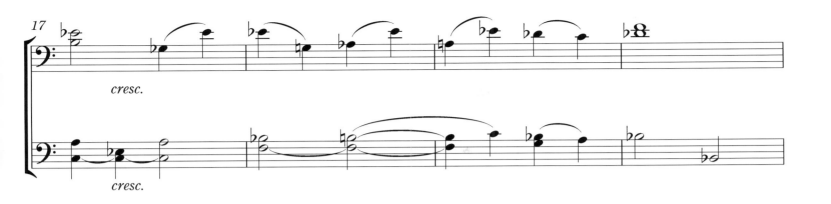

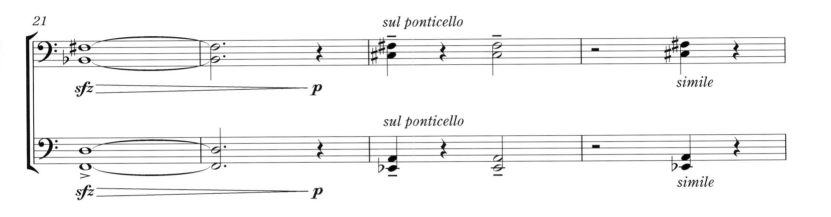

Pièce Lyrique

Questions Réponses

Staccato Legato

TangoCello

Un Adieu

Tarantelle

Slightly faster

Valse de Loretta

TRACK LISTING

CD1
(FULL PERFORMANCE DEMONSTRATIONS)

1. A CLOCHE-PIED
2. ANDANTE
3. BALADE SUR L'EAU
4. BARCAROLLE
5. BORDEAUX MENTHE
6. IMPROVISATION
7. ELÉGIE
8. LE BEAU RÔLE
9. LE HÉRISSON
10. PETITE MARCHE
11. PAS DE DEUX
12. PETITE ETUDE
13. PIZZICATI
14. PRÉLUDE
15. PROCESSION
16. PIÈCE LYRIQUE
17. QUESTIONS RÉPONSES
18. STACCATO LEGATO
19. TANGOCELLO
20. UN ADIEU
21. TARANTELLE
22. VALSE DE LORETTA

CD2
(PRACTICE TRACKS)

1. A CLOCHE-PIED
2. A CLOCHE-PIED
3. ANDANTE
4. ANDANTE
5. BALADE SUR L'EAU
6. BALADE SUR L'EAU
7. BARCAROLLE
8. BARCAROLLE
9. BORDEAUX MENTHE
10. BORDEAUX MENTHE
11. IMPROVISATION
12. IMPROVISATION
13. ELÉGIE
14. ELÉGIE
15. LE BEAU RÔLE
16. LE BEAU RÔLE
17. LE HÉRISSON
18. LE HÉRISSON
19. PETITE MARCHE
20. PETITE MARCHE
21. PAS DE DEUX
22. PAS DE DEUX
23. PETITE ETUDE
24. PETITE ETUDE
25. PIZZICATI
26. PIZZICATI
27. PRÉLUDE
28. PRÉLUDE
29. PROCESSION
30. PROCESSION
31. PIÈCE LYRIQUE
32. PIÈCE LYRIQUE
33. QUESTIONS RÉPONSES
34. QUESTIONS RÉPONSES
35. STACCATO LEGATO
36. STACCATO LEGATO
37. TANGOCELLO
38. TANGOCELLO
39. UN ADIEU
40. UN ADIEU
41. TARANTELLE
42. TARANTELLE
43. VALSE DE LORETTA
44. VALSE DE LORETTA

On the odd-numbered tracks you can hear Cello 1 as the prominent part.

On the even-numbered tracks you can hear Cello 2 as the prominent part.